P9-ARM-008

Illustrated by
ADRIENNE ADAMS

HOUSES *from the* SEA

by
ALICE E. GOUDEY

CHARLES
SCRIBNER'S
SONS
New York

To my friend David

This book published simultaneously in the
United States of America and in Canada –
Copyright under the Berne Convention

G-7-66 (CLJ)

Printed in the United States of America
LIBRARY OF CONGRESS CATALOG CARD NUMBER 59-6932

AUTHOR'S NOTE

As you walk along the edge of the sea you may find a shell lying on the sand or on a rocky shore. You stoop and pick it up. How beautiful it is, this "house" of many colors! It seems a pity to part with such a pretty thing, and so, you put it in your pocket. Going farther down the beach you find another shell—and then, still another one; each prettier than the one before. Soon your pockets bulge with your seashell treasure. This is the beginning of your shell collection.

Collecting shells and finding out about the animals that use them for homes is one of the nicest hobbies in the world.

Shells belong to different family groups just as we do. In this book we have chosen shells from family groups whose members may be found on the eastern, the western and the gulf coasts of our country. For instance, scallop shells, whose family name is Pectinidae, may be found on the east and west coast beaches as well as the beaches of the gulf coasts.

You may not be as fortunate as the children in this book; you may not find them all in one day or all in one place. But at one time or another the tides and the storms will leave them on the beaches.

In this book we have used the common names for the shells. But when you start collecting them you should learn the scientific names, also. Shell books in your public library will tell you their scientific names and how to collect land shells, fresh water shells and seashells, and how to clean and store them.

When we took our pails and shovels
and went down to the sea
the waves ran up to meet us
as if glad that we had come.
They made a fizzing, bubbling sound
as the lacy edges of white foam
swirled around our feet.
And then
the sea rolled back down the beach.
My sister called to it;
she called to it and said,
"Come back!
Oh, please come back and play with us!"

As if it heard her call
the sea came running back.
But

again it slipped away
as if pulled back down the beach
by some hand we could not see.
Even though our friend, the sea,
did not stay and play
it brought in treasures
and left them lying on the sand for us.
We found two moon shells
so smooth and round
they fitted in our hands.
The little animals that once lived inside the shells,
and used them for their homes,
were gone:
the shells were ours to keep—
these little houses that came in from the sea.
We put the moon shells in our pails
and then

another wave came rolling in.
We watched a spotted sandpiper,
out hunting bugs and Hippa crabs,
run before the wave
on tiny match-stick legs.

When the sea
slipped back down the beach
we found some tiny wedge shells,
with colors so gay and pretty,
they looked as if a dozen butterflies
had come to rest their wings
beside the sea.
And then, again

the sea climbed up the beach.
This time it left
a row of dainty jingle shells.
Silver!
Gold!
And apricot!
The colors of the jingle shells
were beautiful and bright.
These little shells
made a merry, tinkling sound
when we put them in our pails.

The next treasures that we found
were the prettiest ones of all—
angel wings,
so beautiful and white,
it seemed they must have come
straight down from heaven.

And then we saw some cockle shells
with ridges, like small ribs,
on their backs.
We touched the edges of the cockles;
they felt like sharp-toothed saws.
When we put two shells together
they made a little heart-shaped house.
And next we found

some precious cowrie shells.
Their rounded sides were smooth and shiny
and speckled with white dots.
Along the opening in the shells
were rows of tiny teeth.
I've been told that many years ago
the yellow cowrie shell
was used for money
just as we use
gold and silver.

We looked beneath the seaweed
washed up on the beach,
and there we found
some keyhole limpets.
We thought they looked like
Chinese hats
with tiny keyholes
in the tops.

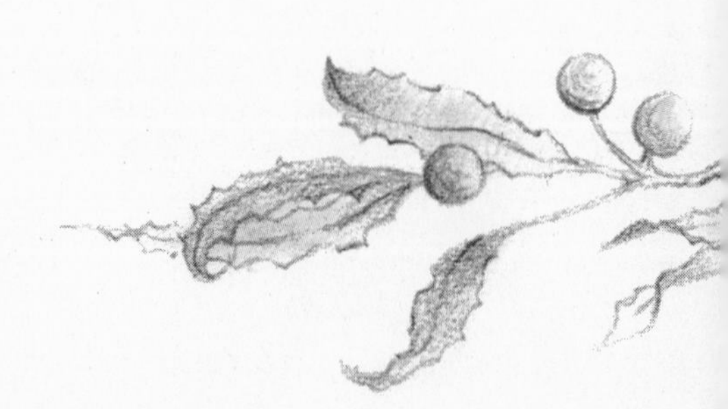

Tangled in the seaweed
we found some periwinkle shells.
We knew that snails
once lived inside these little houses.

We saw some white shells
lying on the sand.
They had such a funny sounding name
that we sang it over and over,
"Wentletraps, wentletraps, wentletraps!
Oh, we have found
some wentletraps!"
This funny name is a Dutch word.
It means a spiral staircase.

We wondered if some wee folk of the sea
used these shells
for stairways in their houses.

The next shells that we found
were scallop shells
with crimpy edges.
They were shaped like ladies' fans,
with little ridges
from top to bottom.

And then we picked up shells
that looked as if they might
spin round and round.
They were top shells,
pointed at one end
and trimmed with little beaded cords.

We found some slipper shells
lying on the dark, wet sand.
I'm sure a water sprite
could wear these little shells
for slippers.
They had little half-decks
across one end,
so we pretended they were boats
sailing on the sea.

We hunted farther along the beach
and there we came upon some shells
that were very different from all the others
we had found.
They were slender turret shells.
We thought they looked like
towers on some old-time castle
but some people think
they look like screws
with spiral ridges swirling round them.
And next

we found some clam shells
with tiny ridges on their rounded backs
like widening circles in a pool of water.
The shells were lined with pearly white
and trimmed with purple edges.
The Indians called the clams that once lived inside
these thick, hard shells
quahogs.

The Indians made pretty, polished beads
of white and purple
from the quahog shells.
They called the little beads "wampum"
and used them for money
when trading with the white men.

They made necklaces and belts and collars
from the small shell beads
and gave them,
as gifts of peace,
to the early settlers of our country.

I heard the mewing of a gull
as it flew above my head.
I heard the deep voice of a boat
far out at sea.
And then I heard my sister's voice.
"Oh, look!" my sister called.
"I see a shell that's walking!"
I looked and saw
a moon shell moving across the sand.

A hermit crab
had crawled inside the shell
and was using it for his home.
As he moved across the beach
he carried his shell house on his back.
As we watched
he seemed to look at us
with bulging eyes.
I told my sister that the hermit crab
had crawled inside the shell
because he had no hard shell of his own
to cover the soft part of his body.
I told her that when he grew bigger
he would find his moon shell house too small.
Then he would go hunting for a larger shell
in which to make his home.

The last shells that we found
were the biggest
and the best of all.
They were whelk shells
with large openings on their sides.
We held these openings to our ears
and listened.
It seemed as if we could hear
the whole song of the sea
coming from within the shells;
the far-off roar of waves,
the soft whisperings,
the stronger sound of wind and surf.
Oh, we were glad that we had found these shells
that seemed to hold the song
the sea sings all day long.

And now the sun was going down;
the day was ending.
The tide was coming in;
the water from the sea
was covering up the beach.
Our pails were full
so we went home
with all our treasures.

When friends come in
to play on rainy days
we show them all our shells.
We tell their names,
just where we found them,
and all about the day
the waves ran up to meet us.

angel wings
wedge shell
slipper shell
top shell
moon shell
turret shell
cockle shell
clam shell

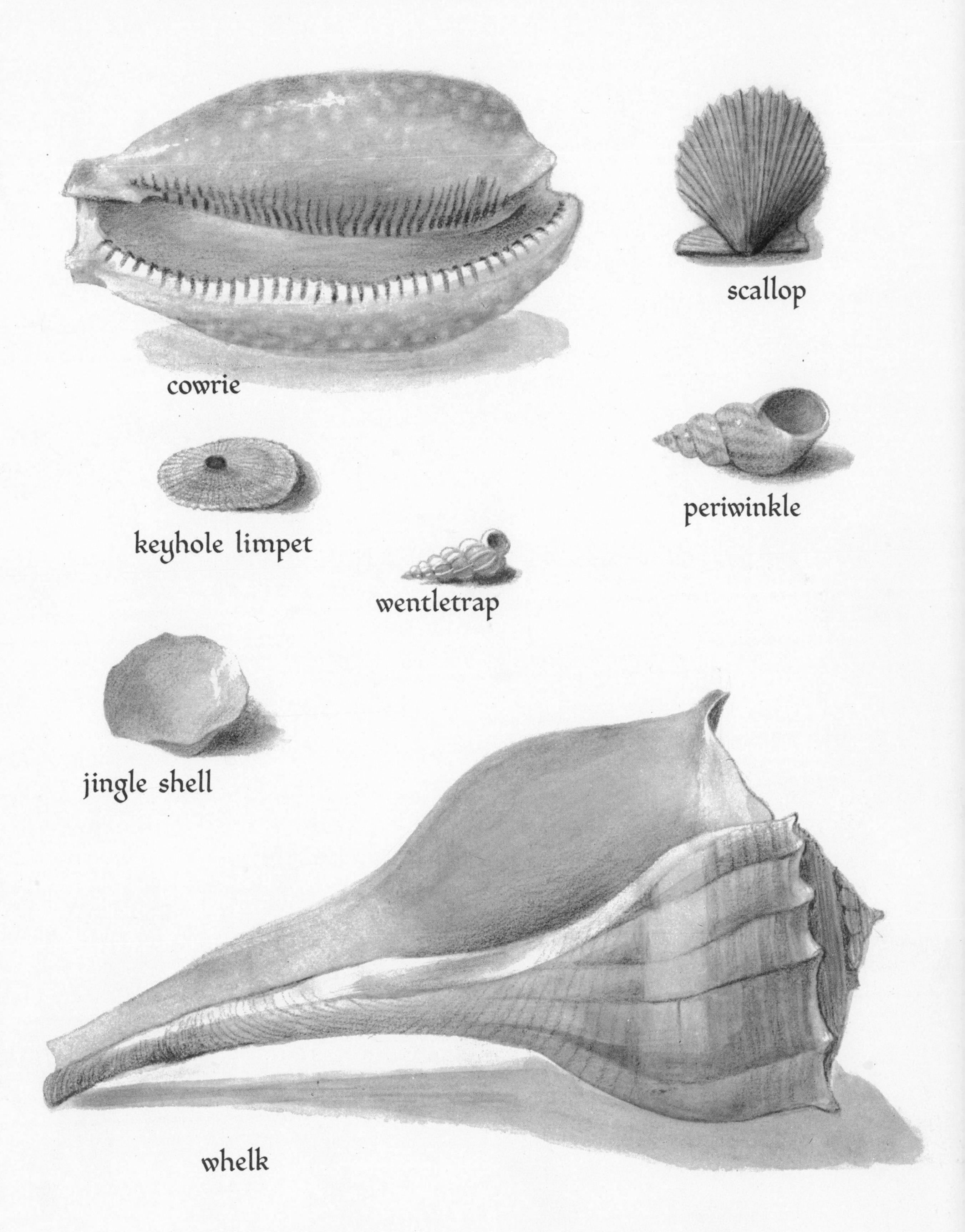
scallop
cowrie
periwinkle
keyhole limpet
wentletrap
jingle shell
whelk

I'm sure that I could never build
a house as beautiful
as these little houses
that the animals of the sea
built for themselves.
So many different kinds;
so many different colors.
Each kind of animal
made the house
that served him best.
I hope, when we go back another day,
our friend, the sea,
will bring more shell houses
and leave them on the beach for us.

HOW SHELLS ARE MADE

Sometimes you may find shells on the beach that have live animals inside of them. This is especially true if you find them soon after a storm at sea has washed them ashore.

The shells, together with the animals that live inside the shells, are called mollusks.

Most baby mollusks hatch out of eggs that have come from inside their mother's bodies.

A mollusk does not have a backbone. Its body is very soft. So, while it is still tiny, it starts to build a hard shell that will protect its soft body from enemies and the rough sea waves. Some mollusks start to build their shell houses while they are still inside the egg.

Some mollusks make their shells all in one piece, or valve. These shells are called univalves. "Uni" means "one". The shells of whelks and snails are made all in one piece and are called univalves.

Other mollusks, such as clams and scallops, make shells that have two parts, or valves. These two-piece shells are called bivalves. "Bi" means "two". The two parts, or pieces, are hinged together at the back. When you pull the outer edges apart the shell opens like a book.

A special part of the mollusk's body does the work of shell-building. This special part is called the mantle.

The mantle is a sac of thin skin that covers most of the soft body of the mollusk. It lies between the body and the shell.

You may see a part of the mantle along the outer edge of some shells. It sometimes looks like a frilly ruffle and is often a beautiful bright color.

The material for building the shell oozes out of the mantle. This material soon hardens and forms the covering that we call the shell. Day by day, as the soft body of the mollusk grows larger, the mantle adds more building material which hardens and makes the shell grow larger, too. Coloring material also oozes from the mantle and colors the shell with bright patterns.

A large part of the material that oozes from the mantle is made from carbonate of lime. This material makes the shell hard. The mollusk gets the carbonate of lime from its food in much the same way we get building material from our food to make our bodies grow.

In this way all of the "houses from the sea" with their ribs and scallops, their many different shapes and their different color patterns were made by the animals that once lived inside of them.

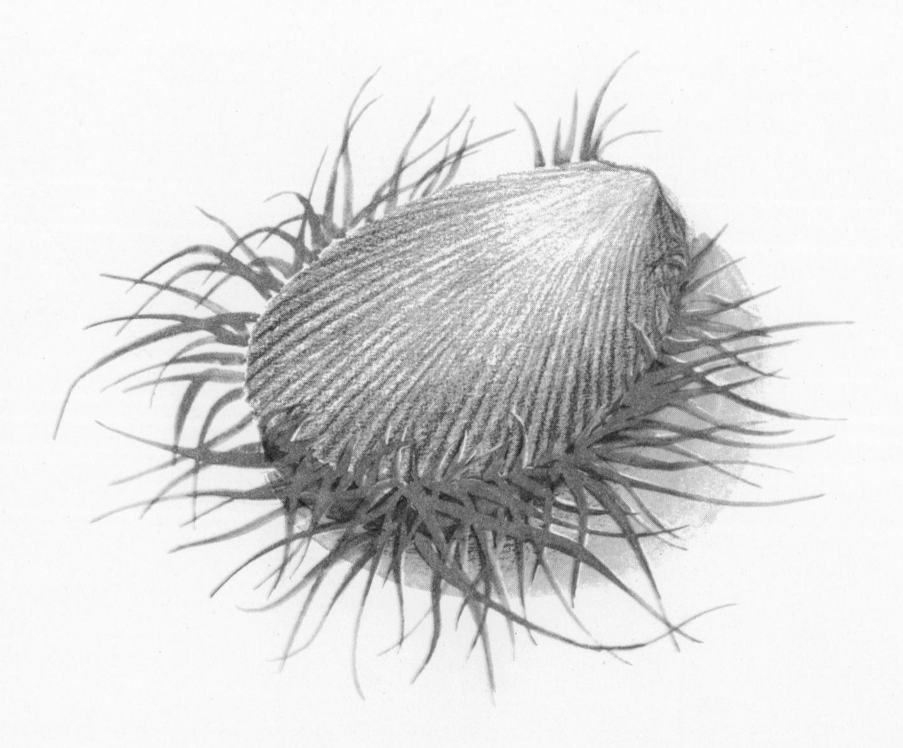